HOLY HARLOTS

SANDEEP DAHIYA

For all those who came and left unsung.

O Mother,

My first footstep lies in thy womb,

From such a start how can I go wrong?

Contents

Contents

Foreword

These are the heart-felt songs which in fact have been the poet's companions during the toughest phase in his life. Most of these have been written in the charming countryside of the poet's native place at a small village in northern India. The poems try to capture the softest nuances of perceptible and imperceptible naturalities against the background of human trials and tribulations. The verses chime with an enamouring softness of the heart which sound Godsent against the present times viciously self-obsessed noise. The poems are exceptionally laced with silent spiritual reflections over the comforting quietude and teasing tranquility of the countryside. These simple swathes of aesthetics take the reader to a slow-paced world...far, far away from the 'maddening crowd'!

Acknowledgements

Of all the people, I acknowledge the deeply humanistic impressions ingrained in me through ideal upbringing by my father Late Shri Ran Singh Dahiya; unconditional love and care showered on me by my mother Late Smt. Shakuntla Devi; fathomless affection shown by my sisters Manju and Sudesh; endless support and faith by my brother Amit and his wife Poonam.

I feel blessed with the unconditional love of my nephew Nevaan and nieces Saifiya and Maira.

Holy Harlots

Yamuna!

A black, toxic, putrefied *nullah*.

Cow!

A sewage-eating big pig

surviving on garbage dumps.

Two holy mothers turned harlots

in this age of *Kaliyuga*!

Delhi, meanwhile, pumps

more pride in its polluted lungs.

On stinking sewage-layered banks,

The skinny cow grazes on

noxious weeds and poisoned shrubbery,

Its beneficent, teary eyes

ogle at the human-industrial waste

mocking and mirthing over Yamuna's sighs.

Who needs a holy bath now and cow's blessings?

Two pillars of faith

now crumble down to pieces,

Any listeners to their dismantling shrieks?

Holy Touch!

With softly pining majesty, silence sings a song,
Shadows grow long,
Her soft fingers brace my face
and go along a teary trace.
Delicate tip of her finger bears the jewel,
The tear that would have been lost as salt on my face.

Phoenix

In the fire of my passion

people say I will burn my wings,

And then I will not be able to fly,

How mischievously society takes a dig sly

at those who dare to be different,

For rutted path's stranglehold is luring,

doling out short-cuts aiming massive gains,--

The ordinary paths avoiding the penanceful pains.

Burn I'll myself in my own fire

to ashes and ambers,

Or the inferno will bake the skill raw

To turn gold in my soul's chambers,

Either ashes or gold—

Though the path full of miseries untold,

But even this treacherousness has exceptional charms,

Its forlorn sand is pregnant with virginal solitude,

Its uncluttered loneliness, a mine full of possibilities!

Far away from the crowd

How brilliantly shines that prospect!

The solitary walkers on this path

either die a lonely, ignominious death,

To become the unencumbered particles of its ungutted earth,

Or if somebody carries through the desert,

He arrives at an oasis of gold,

where the creative bliss takes him in charming fold.

These sufferings might turn me into ashes

or turn me into gold,

If the ash is my fate

then I should not hate

my passion's flame,

For I turned out to be a horse lame

that lined up for the toughest race,

Or with inferno lurking in my face

I play with the fire

and make it my mistress to sire

the golden-winged off-springs;

my consummation signs with the infernal *houri*,

That wedding night's taming with creative fury.

The moth is aware of the fire's fury,

Still it doesn't hover

around a desirous flower's utility,

With passionate ambers smoldering in its guts,

It goes for a dazzling display around the fire;

Its perilous, exciting, flirtatious orbit around the glow,

And the flame laying snares for the deadly blow,

Yet with intoxicated zeal

nearer and nearer it comes to kiss and feel

that finest nectar hidden behind the fiery eyes:

The honey sweeter than any flower

for which a worldly honey-bee dies.

Fuelled and fired by every ounce of its instinct

it buzzes around with ecstatic swirls,

It lives life thousand times more

than the ones lured by worldly flower's lore,

Even its death isn't just painful plights,

It is merely the pinnacle of its

gradually graduating love flights,

And when it meets its end that explosion of its flesh

is the acme of its fiery passion.

Likewise, I'm the helpless satellite

of the sun of my art,

Hardest I might try,

but from it I can't part,

It's my life and source of light,

Without it everything is a blind flight

and nothing of purpose in sight,

Hovering around my inspirational sun

is the only form of my fun,

Even if it means the final

Crash-landing into the fiery ball,

For the artist it still is a regally carpeted hall.

Mirage

How possessed the show of life floats away!

Self-absorbed and self-satiating eyes

perpetually ogling at that last ray,

Shines which with trayful of exceptional mundanities,

delicious crumbs and specks of pleasant trivialities,--

Prize's lesser essence exaggerated manifold,

How deceiving has'n this mirage since times untold!

The rioting mob, meanwhile, creating a stampede and storm—

Thirsty, hungry, eating and breathing sand,

Trying to outpace one another

to reach that coveted oasis land,

where the mirageful sweet speck lies

and the supposed spring of will never dries.

God created us to walk brotherly

on the lush green pastures hand-in-hand,

But we take the path lost in treacherous sand

to out-run others,

Leaving others dying

and lying to be buried under those sand dunes,

So much we lose and force others to lose

while running to catch those boons,

Blindly we trample orchids

to catch up with the call by those sandy sighs,

And see, so many die with sand in mouth and eyes!

See that fellow huffing and puffing like an animal

going after that ever-escaping destination,

Like a bull sweating out the precious drops

to drain out even the last ounces of vitality

from those strained innards,--

The orchid inside suffers a drought,

Aah! How valiantly he fought,

But unfortunately always had'n taking unnecessary shot,

And then the chase became unbearably hot,

Desire's hallucination sparkles in his eyes as the loser's blot.

Ever pretending to kow-tow the pious injunctions,

most often we do the opposite,

How coquettishly we keep God

unaware of our motives true!

The characters outsmarting the creator's real hue,

Betraying thus God and trampling orchards,

whose seeds He planted in us,

we move ahead,

Unaware the spirit is already dead,

And the title deed with the creator

torn and tattered to its last thread,

Then we go out without any dread

and tread over each other in blind race,

Spit each other in the face

to stop (or made to stop) finally at a place,

where there isn't that presumption's single trace.

Highway Murder

Listen you all, men and nature!

They are killing me!

As the iron hisses and kisses

the rings of my age,

I stand benumbed in daze,

This end was not supposed to come so soon,

Wasn't I fulfilling all the duties assigned to me,

entitling me another wintery full moon?

In self-imposed anesthesia

I just feel the saw's butchering

in the bloodless flesh in my guts,

There is no blood in me

to give the evidence of a murder,

The sanguine darkness of my mass

is worth only stone for you.

On this hazily sun-lit winter noon,

The hounds are around me,

My murder has been sanctioned

by the state authorities!

For decades I stood for both nature and man,

During those beautiful days

this road was a simple friend

leading to common journeys and destinations,

Now it becomes a foe and highway

leading to some illustrious ray,

And I become redundant old,

standing in the way of progress

with my few square-feet of foot-hold.

If a healthy mass like me is no life;

no more than a mile-stone,

I hope to tell my murder story

till the axes, scythes and saws

send my tiniest of branches to be turned to ashes.

We trees never wince with pain

as your axes spray around chips of our flesh,

I understand we had equal rights

till mankind was just part of the nature,

Now this saw going deeper and deeper

into my bloodless guts,

reminds me of our inevitable fate,--

Every tree on earth now has a deadly date

with the greedy most, treacherous and unforgiving mate.

They know that I'm massive and big,

So they are afraid of my fall,

Haa! The cowards!

They don't know, while they rob me

of my few square feet of space on earth,

My saplings are still doling out oxygen

under this winter sun,

Even my murder can't change me

because I'm helpless due to my nature.

Now the saw has gone sufficiently deep,

And I get some signs of that eternal sleep,

I feel some unbearable pain in my painless mass,

For death is death after all,

Hope you will understand!

Like hangman's noose, thick hemp ropes

are tied to direct my fall,

From a safe distance, the tractors pull

to bring down this wooden bull,

And now I feel the pain

as cleavage breaks through that portion

still holding me to my mother earth,

From softest saplings to rock hard tissues

my whole body is panicked,

Saplings are crying like purely innocent children,

Hardest of trunk tissues are shamelessly crying

like battle hard, handsome soldiers after losing a battle,

But who cares!

This big snapping sound is my death cry,

And I fall with a thud,

Yes, man you win,

I'm dead before I thought I will!

Spring Seeds

…and now the April has also gone,

Where are the seeds that I'd sown?

Like a ploughman I worked

in the summer almost melting bones,

Removed the stones,

Rattled which the spirit like someone

caught in desert's sandy moans.

Then during winter my toil lit up a bonfire

amidst blinding blizzards and nature's icy deeds,

These were my spring seeds,

embedded, impregnated in earth through my earthy deeds,

Spring seeds meant to

conceive, germinate, grow, ripe, flower and fructify,

But the spring came and went with a sad sigh,

Sorrows in my barren fields hit another high,

My spring seeds thus lost,

And me the farmer standing forlorn

without that harvest of which I used to boast,

Now the scorching May sun

beats down the dusty land with a fiery pun,

Peasant and his field thus stand mute,

Almost complete has'n the plunder and loot,

To gallows was sent my crop,

The hangman just mechanically pulled

the handle at the hanky's drop,

Efforts' dead body hangs from that noose,

And even the last strains of

faith, will power and hope getting loose.

People say that too much is my browbeat,

‘Why not clear another stony plot

to get something to eat?’

Perhaps they don’t realize

the blind, illogical passion’s treatise

which I wrote over stones with a pure soul,

Impractical, insane I stand out

with cracks and brain’s hole,

How could I expect fruits from this very plot?

And now I stare at the nullifying blot,

The desert storm meanwhile hisses with its lust hot,

Seeds have most probably been killed,

Aah, with amazing precision

the Goddess of infertility drilled!

While the songs of my fertile efforts in a chorus trilled,

But She has’n successful in its swipe,

Its blinding gung-ho and macabrous hype,

Lolloping its greedy tongue to

dejuice and deflower everything ripe,

Now I lay my back against a

hard, hot, unshaded rock,

My weariness, fatigue and torture

put me in a sleepy dock,

In that short uneasy sleep

I get some relief from the pain of this injury deep,

A luxuriant crop I see in my dream

and nearby gurgling goes a stream.

The Invisible, Untouched Debris

A painful churning goes on

in the deep, deep recesses mine,

Outwardly I manage to look well and fine.

On my skin sweat beads shine,

These tiny outpours of my desperation

are the struggling vestiges of battles

that I failed to win.

There is a salty sea of sufferings inside,

which the clothing and the mask hide,--

The sea of tears accumulated from yores,

Here mournful, tragic waves strike

the forlorn sand on gloomy shores,

There were deep, hollow pits and spaces

that could have'n easily filled up with

sweet freshwaters and lifeful braces,

But that wasn't to be,

Rather the tears of endless traumas

made up the sorrowful sea,

Outwardly I just tread on the ground,

And even try to dance

to the social puppetry and civilized sound,

But in the deep recesses of the sea of my being

sharks shred the flesh like the bloodiest of hound,

Thousands of leeches suck the soul's blood,

And the salty sea gets another torrential flood,

Surrounded by such deadly gloomy waters,

My being's lofty peaks

shudder with protesting shrieks,

In those vales, precipitation born of miseries

sends down dark showers,

Creating mudslides and breaking stones

from the lofty towers,

Deep echoes of this sea's triumphant storms

go rumbling through the inner being,

Rains, floods, earthquakes

storm the soul's citadel,

Their combined fury unleashes mud and sleaze,

Carries which the ensnaring breeze

towards the salty sea of gloom,

Even though outwardly I manage to

keep up some bloom,

But the tremors from inside

reach new high day by day,

And the scared soul runs helter-skelter

to find some solacing ray

that might say

a valiant nay

to the horrible avalanche pouncing on my soul,

But unmindfully the rocks of

my ideas and principles fatally slide,

and painfully the debris glide

towards the salty sea.

If the erosion from inside

goes on like this,

while I try to maintain the appearance

worth a lady's kiss,

Then it will leave a huge

cavern overlooking the sea,

Collapse it will then,

And that shiny façade and that wren

will crash with its glittering,

broken eyeglasses still facing the sky,

With the last imprint of final worldly

shot with a cry,

What difference will it make then?

Perhaps, people will still

shed tears over the shiny shell,

And muse,

'He didn't die as a broken man.

He was as starry as anyone can!'

Their analysis will just

mull over the debris shiny,

But nobody will give solace

to the agonic corrosion going inside,

Because those who couldn't

see it while I was alive,

How can they now

when I take the final dive?

Obituary lines will be written

on those broken shiny shards;--

Farcical symbols of my worldly struggle

and puny success,

While the real struggle

thousand times valorous remains unsung,

For it lies scattered at the lowest rung,

What foolhardiness!

Soul's sanctorum halls

remain in deadly pals,

while they kiss only the temple's

outer walls.

Golden Noose

With that invisible love story

tied with an unseen cord

to my tightly sewn lips,

Let me kiss the last drops of her memory

from the cup still brimming

with her image.

The last spiritual door

opening finally for His light,

Preparing for something more,

somewhere in some other world and form,

Where down the distanceless

space-time continuum

lies the timeless face of an

untold, unrequited love tale.

The tiny waves of breathing

can now no longer carry the boat of life,

Last moment's stormy seizure

quickly subdues the feeble efforts to stay afloat,

And down goes the body,

Hanged by the cord

of a painful love story that was never told.

The Defeated King

The night was very long

and all moments thronged

with frustration, angst and despair,

The darkest faces yelled for anyone to dare.

Like a terribly lynched mule

sluggered away the day

without bringing a new ray,

Now, the night's long sinewy hairs

cast ghastly shadows over the battlefield lost,

And battle scars get bandaged with frost.

A cumbersome long-long day

when his efforts got butchered

by some mysterious force's riotous ray,

Now stars shine on darkness' face;

Like tiny lamps they twinkle from

some fallen hero's mace

and point to hope and smile

somewhere still holding onto tiniest of trace,

Their poking raylets brace

the frozen blood around scars,

'The day will come', they say,

'and the next sun will light up a new ray!'

'You will then forget these days dark

and still fearsome nights with a terrible hark!'

The wounded, handsome soldier's hands

clenched a fistful of earth all blood-soiled,

There were more moments to be toiled,

Somewhere fire in his blood still boiled,

The enemy'll return in a couple of hours,

'Let me see how many heads my club covers!'

For the mace handle his hands fumbled,

But once again his feet stumbled

and he fell down,

But that effort's majesty shone on his face,

Succumbed he then to his injuries and died,

Aha! Immortal was that last shot of pride,

It was found frozen on his face

when the victorious hound

arrived later on the trophy's trace.

Invisible Scars

Too often I've stumbled, staggered

and fallen headlong,

Cuts and wounds mercilessly throng

the bodily stranglehold mine,

Deep fissures reach

where the soul's diamonds shine;

Injuries so deep—

Aaah! Invisible, invincible dragnet's richest reap.

Nobody sees the gaping holes in my spirit,

Here the destiny's blind force

so venomously hit!

God! Why is it that deepest scars

are invisible to the society's eyes?

Why remain unnoticed

cuts and wounds of such mammoth size?

Injuries like deepest trenches on the sea's bosom,

Above on the surface

the worldly water waves normally,

Below the scars lurk dreadfully

and darkest of the dark roam

in the gloomy, depthless womb.

I, the perpetual peasant,

Always engaged in the sacred labour duty,

While the foe doing

its undoing spadework continuously,

Its ensnaring checkerwork grinning cunningly,

I meanwhile rise up again

to get some littlest bit of gain,

Alas, my mountainously bulky efforts

only but go haywire!

Not even a little tick or mite I find,

And sorrowfully the tiny lamp goes blind,

The invisible scars

get enlarged and multiplied, of course,

But not even a single eye

sees the bloody bath and the loss!

Last Hideout

Here I sit in my cold, secluded corner

and take stock of the

pleasant profanities scattered around,

The world basking in its

majestic, unholy mundanities,

while the unhindered morality singing unbound.

The corner with its stagnant stench

and mucking air;

where my tortured holy-self lie,

Cruelly contriving world meanwhile tempts,

'Why thou become the fodder of game fair?

Son, now have an unfair try!'

'Succeed thou will,

the moment thou unshackle

thyself of poor righteousness!

This load will always find you a loser,

for too old is now the history of uprightness!'

And I shiver and snivel

in my little, dark hole

to keep the little flicker going,

The dark race however gets

perpetually stormy and cries,

'Let's us see! How long you'll keep rowing?'

Too small is the boat which carries me

across this deadly sea,

Big waves pound from all sides

and each crest devilishly neigh.

How foolish of me

not to surrender to the cozy

seduction by the compromising short-cut!

Cut after cut they give me

to break open my little hutment

whose wispy door is bravely shut.

Passes as the time,

graver still become the urgency to

drag me out of my hiding hole,

Too far and wide is the

swash of 'only feasible game'

in which all must play a survival role.

God! Let me see how long I can cling

to my altar-like holy den,

But times are really dark

and the moment will surely come,

The little lamp will go blind then···

Birth

This tiny flower

becoming a fruit;--

Transformation of this

once petalous soot:

Its beauty and colour

now turning into a tiny vase,

Old flower and the infant fruit

transmixing for the nature's laws.

Flower's beauty being sacrificed

at the fruity altar,

The Goddess of fruits

watches this pleasant hatching from far,

She muses with a midwifery glee,

Sings then a playful lullaby for the

fruitling in the flower's womb,

Oh! How glittery is this little juicy lad

in the petalous tomb.

So, the soft flowery curls

take a hard, fruity mould,

The petals bold

turn into juicy, hard fold.

Love Storm

When love smiles like a rose,

some famished heart gets a dose,

Cupid's arrow breaks the shackles

and that unemotional, hard crust crackles.

A pumping machine is heart no longer,

as the softest turbulence gets stormily stronger,

Love storm knocks at the rugged coastline,

There for a new dawn, several suns shine.

The Love like a flower

sways to sizzling dew shower,

Dew-drenched, a new life sizzles,

and moments rejuvenate in precious drizzle.

The heart dancing in the rain,

Pleasant madness; nothing to gain!

Sheer abundance of all giving,

Gain-lorn is no longer the being.

Heart's orchard in full bloom,

Archaic-old now seems that gloom,

Brightly starry is the night,

Self-esteem soars to loftiest height,

And when the storm ebbs out,

like a panicked fish the heart's angels shout,

'Oh, thou uncertain tide,

when will thou again arrive with thy sweep wide?'

The Game

How hard and how long

I take to reach near

the summit of my hardworked hill,

All battered and bruised,

final steps I still try,

Above, the peak brags its highness,

while the caterpillar's soul doth cry:

'Yonder, still uphill sweet cups lie!'

My eyes ogle at the peak,

And heart ready to render

a full-throated victorious shriek,

But eyes then see

the hard taskmaster's glee,

Awaits who there to teach

that solacing sips are still out of reach.

Oh! Its quick ascendancies!

Always galloping ahead

with mammoth mirth in hand,

It is always the first

to quench its thirst

from the cup at the crest,

Then uproariously beats its breast:

'There lies another one!

Pal, let's get promptly begun!'

Oofs, its insatiable thirst!

It claims exulting victory every time,

And I get my weeping, mediocre rhyme.

The 1412th Toy

So they are clapping for their achievement!

They are celebrating the 1412th tiger in this land

where my forefathers roamed to make legends.

But before they take all the credit

for saving my species,

Let me—a mere skinny kitten—clarify:

A tiger born in a zoo is no tiger!

An animal opening its eyes for the first time

among self-vaunting humans is no animal,

It's a mere flesh and blood toy

conceived by semi-dark conscience

and mechanical techniques.

No man! No I'm no tiger!

I'm just a tiny means to allow you mighty

people to get some solace,

The genes in me have been broken

through your rampages across my lands,

You people know me as a mighty

hunter galloping after my prey,

And here in the confines of this cage

My parents forgot that they were tigers,

Your cages just define we poor animals

Just as poor dependents,

The showcase items for your kids,

To be hooted at,

To be laughed at,

To be mocked at,

No man no! I am no tiger!

I'm just a proof of

you outgrowing your shoes,

What tiger is a tiger that is tame,

It hangs down its tail in shame,

Yes man, you win!

And I bear the burden of being a tiger,

even though my genes have been changed!

Kiss of Death

Life! My purest kisses on your lips

were the honest stamps of

genuine love and loyalty,

I was in supremely pure love,

Even though my delicate, soft smooches

were returned by you as bleeding bites,

I always smiled,

ascending higher and higher to loftiest delights.

Each moment found me unprecedently crazy,

infatuated and caught in the sweet

tentacles of unreined, unrestrained love,

You but always bit back more viciously,

Oh thou heartless seductress!

Taking the poison as sweetest honey,

with bleeding lips I always smiled,

Cuts after cuts you gave,

even before the previous blood dried.

You only sucked,

I just gave rosy hues to you,

and you returned deadly blue,

Still smile and sweetness never

left my bloody lips,

How crazily I shed those lifeful drips!

Blindly I surrendered my *being* before you,

And you tricked me,

for I always saw life in that deadly hue.

Greedily gasping with venomous sighs and winner's hiss,

You now approach with that final kiss

to deprive me of the final breaths,

Life! Aren't you ashamed of cheating someone

who perhaps loved you the most?

Flying Kiss

In these slumberous vales

and shy, silent dales,

My spirit escapes the clutch-hold

of my confined being,

And ecstatically saunters away

to those snow-melting peaks,

where the March sun breastfeeds

many a tiny rivulets,

Like a helpless, rooted palm,

I assuage myself and put balm

on my constricted conscience,

Cold sighs I vent out,

as the pinnacled majesty winks

from far with a seductive pout,

And my forlorn spirit runs amok

and flies to kiss those

coyly surrendering, shining crystals,--

Away, away where rock's snobby

ego melts maternally!

A Plump Hatch, and Tiny Catch

The day rose

after that stand-still, dark pause,

Like an infant's mysterious muse,

pinkish horizon took shape

with dreams huge.

Warmth and light rapidly spread,

Light prevailed and darkness retreated

with an uncharacteristic dread,

Shadows first lengthened

and then shrank to become bold;

clung firmly to get noontime foothold.

With crowning majesty,

the moments moved towards the zenith,

Everything warmed for brightest glory,

With a firmly straight venture

written was that glorious story,

Roses, roses all the way,

Endless seemed that ray,

Meanwhile the pendulum

swung the other way,

During the lazy afternoon's lugubrious sway,

shadows silently crept away,

In that slumberous silence,

many a leaves gave away

to the titillating pulls of

mother earth's gravity song,

Shadows panicked and slowly-slowly

ebbed away to become long,

The other horizon now crimson and red,

It sprayed colours sad,

Lolloping tongues of its funeral fury,

firmed up like death sentencing jury,

Tired voices, slow steps, ebbing strength:

The day that had risen

with such pomp and show,

It was wiped away after that

feeble twilight 'no' .

Criminal Moment

There were times

and there would be times,

But endless is the moment

that still chimes

with the evil song and music of a crime,

A crime when it plucked a life

like a thief sneaking away with last breath

amidst heartbeats missing their mark

imperiled by that chaos and strife.

I bear witness against that murderous moment,

when I was left fatherless and

put on an unprotected plane like never before,

Like a boatman cast away

countless treacherous miles from the shore;

Like a pariah face

Bumping against a slammed, shut door.

No a fatherless being can't be

the same anymore,

Moments will come

and moments will go,

But the steely vessel of my being

is almost cut to depth by that perilous hoe.

Betrayal

Life! You are plainly a treacherous friend,

He loved you more than himself,

Nurtured you with the most potent,

pious and vigorous juices of innocent childhood;

Fattened thy fibers

with the impassioned heartbeats of youth;

Increased the aura around your hallowed head

through graceful wisdom and talks of ripening age.

He made you the charming queen of his dreams,

With decades of love and toil,

he prepared a glittering palace for you,

And then you eloped,

Eloped with dark-winged shadows of death,

You crazy one!

Right from the start you were in

blind love with the angels of death.

Yet all he did was to love you,

Love you from the core of his soul.

Blossomed he a flower

that was always love-lorn for the

ghastly clutch from the other world,

Now, here lies your lover's corpse

and you make merry with your evil playmate,

hidden in the darkest chambers.

Spring Rose

Spring rose!

Pampered by the nights' dewy dose

your full-lipped pout

invites stingy, sucking bites

from the black bee, the lout!

You but mind it not

and give fresh flashes and fragrant shot,

Your lover's impassioned gasps hot,

shake you up like a storm tossing a boat,

You but still smile,

Pure, unstinted, without any guile!

You have the softest, petalous lips,

And like a rapist he just sips

the feminine juices of your blood,

You rosy red and he black,

His crazy, blind passion lets loose a flood,

His darkish, sweating, contorted face,

How murderously he responds

to your innocent, breezy grace!

Greedily he goes on,

Those fiery grunts, subduing your softest moan,

And reaching the dangerous peaks

where his unquenchable thirst shrieks,

The plunderer flies away!

Away! Where more fresh faces sway,

You but still smile,

His love bites prominent on your lovely face,

Aha, undefeatable is this grace!

Vandalized Rose

Full moon night and this pond!

The sky flaunts its full-faced beauty,

The pond too kisses

the mirage, the reflection!

Love-lorn, the gentlest waves

caress the lovely, tricky mirage,

Ducks quack!

From the shore-side bushes

a bird suddenly goes for a night song,

With expert ease

and like nimblest breeze

suddenly a pack of night-fliers arrives,

And the hawks go for a hearty feast,

for every hungry belly is a beast,

Sharp talons, strong beaks, sturdy wings,

The air with pugnacity sings,

They swoop down on the soft delicacies

enjoying the soft bedspread on rippling waves,

That lotus too bears a talon scar,

The birds of prey swoop down for one-sided war,

Soft flesh; rock hard claws,

How easily soft life's skin saws!

There is blood, noise and shrieks,

This softest of solitude creaks

And breaks down

in the tight, lusty embrace of the storm,

A piece of black cloud takes the milky full face

in its dark, mating brace,

There is darkness, blood, bites and noise,

Those dreamful moments lost of their poise!

Now, the oblivious cloud,

free of its impassioned hinges,

flies away, surrendered to the winds,

The sad beauty smiles again,

And throws its tired, tamed milkiness

on this torn serenity and pause,

lying here like a vandalized rose!

Illustrious Sun

He was great in his own ways,

A small but substantial sun

brilliantly scattering its rays

across his being's orbit,

We the planets majestically circling,

Sourced by him and always in debit,

He was fiery

and spun on his axis with copious fury,

His eyes had dreams,

Dreams of all of us becoming stars,

But fate was always at wars,

In the infinite and mysterious cosmic gloom

disposals were always in full bloom,

He and the family spun,

The supreme intelligence had pun for a fun.

We had our fire storms

and titillating, exciting bumps and smooth rides

in our small cozy orbits,

The burning core of his being

sucked fuel from the happiness born of

big dreams of his planets becoming stars,

But dreams are what?

May be they are the pyres in disguise!

In his own fire he collapsed,

From a distance the chunks of his own body

saw him being consumed

by the same fiery tongues

that had zealously chorused his dreams,

There was an explosion,

His pieces were blown into

the depthless void of eternity,

And we the plants,

Shook, sobbed, stopped;

fatherless in our cradling orbits,

With horror and sorrow

we watched the cataclysmic fire,

Then helplessly driven by the cosmic forces,

we were carried ahead by the time's horses.

A Moment Lives, Dies, Becomes Immortal

A dead mouse lies,

Forlornly the April air sighs,

Water in a nearby puddle dries,

A dung-beetle hurriedly tries

to roll its trophy; take home as pies.

There on the infinite, blue calm of the skies,

an eagle air-dives for ecstatic highs,

With death, decay and destruction,

its hunter instinct vies,

From the faded, sunburnt petals of that flower,

the short spring says byes.

Lower and lower the hunter comes,

It eyes the humble measles

a former life has still to offer,

Driven by the expert dynamics of its airy skill,

It goes for the carcass' kill,

Triumphantly it ascends,

The trophy held in its talons,

A sparrow chirps as if crying of murder,

Another bird sounds applauding,

A curious mix:

The nature in qualityless, impersonal fluid.

Unseen a chapter is closed,

The slumberous panorama, meanwhile, dozed.

Tryst with Destiny

To be popular and great

is the biggest bait,

So many of us miss the charming date

to get a favourable alliance

between hard work and fate,

Alas but it's always too late

by the time journey comes to a sudden halt,

The bubble then bursts,

Names and dates turn to ashes,

Unconcerned world goes on

as usual with pompous dashes,

As soon as you become past,

Redundant thy memories turn really fast,

Still we surrender to the bait,

May be it's just our inevitable, humble fate.

The Princess

Many-many full moons ago,

There was a beautiful princess

in a tiny, paradisiacal hill state,

Surrounded by nature's blooms great

her beauty was ever-touching new scales,

Nature spread across far-flung wild trails

sang songs of her majestic beauty,

Slowly-slowly it did its duty

to spread around the tales of her charms,

For miles and miles

her fame could measure distance in arms,

Reached it the ears of a prince far,

whose kingdom had'n at war

with her father's,

And lo! Enough bravado this prince gathers

to set out to look at that famed face,

Seemed he then a futile chaser

running after destiny in a tragic race,

Lovely wild flowers kept on giving her trace,

Untamed breeze came to brace

his young heart and brave, soldierly chest,

Moved he ahead without rest,

After months-long sufferings in the ravines,

he found himself where her star shines,

Wandered he in her kingdom in impersonation,

for so antagonistic was the air in this nation.

Her fame spread more from the mouth's word,

Too precious was this bird

to be ogled by too many eyes,

So desperately he tries

to give solace to his aching eyes,

His pining heart gave suffering, cold sighs,

Then chance showered its bloom

and gone was his heart's gloom,

It was a full moon night

and moon was lit at its fairest bright,

The princess went for a boat ride

in the marvelously calm lake,

His heart shook with a thunderous heart-quake

as he stealthily waited in the shoreline foliage,

Every passing moment gave a new courage,

He was just above

the princess' safe, secret bathing *ghat* of marble sleek,

This white monument gleamed

exotically in the panorama bleak,

Arrived her boat then with her giggling maidens,

His heart was now achingly struggling

against his broad chest,

In filigreed finery she was dressed,

In silent majesty she put her adorable feet

on the gleaming, cool facade by the waterside,

Waves rippled through him with a coquettish chide,

Her hallowed figure glowed distinctly

among her helping ladies,

And before he could think anything,

stony become his whole being,

Her finery no longer covered

her exquisitively carved flesh curves,

That naked fairy jammed his nerves,

That statuesque glow of marble on her skin soft,--

Aha that real life sculpture of

utmost sensuality and symmetry aloft!

Moon-rays deflected off her curves

and panting, pining reached his eyes,

Every moment her moon-sculpted body

acquired new vistas and highs,

Her flowing tresses on her naked back

lustily shook to her head's gentle gyrations,

He couldn't see her face clearly,

but he heard word spoken with mythic softness,

He was, but, dying to see her face,

so closer and closer he came

to fulfill his young heart's only aim,

Alas! He was noticed by her female arm-guards,

Quickly their masculine arms hissed,

Surrounded by trained females

he'd decent chances of escape through a fight,

But how could he blot this night

by testing against females his skill,

Strong ladies advanced on him

with the chances to kill,

Caught he was in this way,

When the next sun came with its curious ray,

his misadventure's word got around,

Shook then her father's throne's ground.

It was the enemy's unforgivable crime,

So sentenced he was to death at his youth's prime,

But kingdoms have inviolable laws,

so his royal blood deserved

the fulfillment of a last wish,

Then how could he miss

the last chance to see her face,

So request he an eye-full brace

of her magical features,

God! Why thou create such bewitching creatures?

He was thus led to the courtyard

below her balcony ornate,

Her sad eyes looked at him without any hate,

The prince too was no less on handsome scale,

On his perfect features a smile loomed pale,

The princess knew that her face had'n the bait,

which could soon seal this life's fate,

Thus fell she at her father's feet

with an utmost, painful entreat,

'Father it was no fault of his,

but is all due to my well-thought kiss,

Stranger this prince is not,

for your daughter secretively tied the knot,

And if you kill him

sorrows and sins would cross ocean's brim,

A father would widow his daughter,

For ages known will be this slaughter,

And if thou still send him to gallows,

certainly another death bellows'.

How could the King let this

darling flower wither away!

So smiled on many fates a new ray,

They were ceremoniously married,

Decades-old animosity was buried,

What beautiful outcome of her wise, petalous step,--

For herself marital bliss

and for two states a friendly kiss!

The Sage

Many-many years ago,

A sage was meditating

on a Himalayan peak,

Majestic dales and solitary vales around

all aglow with the divine streak,

Though the bird chirped songs

and rain poured down in throngs;

In winters, icy cold storms blew

and snow around and over him rue;

In autumn wind-fallen leaves

sailed down with slumberous tumble,

and fruits ripe fell proudly,

adventurously for a juicy pleasant crumble;

In spring, wild flowers fully unfurled

their fragrance and smile,

and honey-bees engaged in

down-to-dusk toil;

Summer's warm days sprayed

Desultory, eerie uneasiness around,

And cool nights proudly embraced

this son with soul heaven-bound,

But he never changed

from his meditative path.

Then on an autumn full moon night,

A fairy was flying amid milky delight,

Her maidenly circles in the air

found the seer in sight,

But even her laughter

and the rustle of her

unbelievably soft dress failed to

break the spell of the engrossed sage,

His exquisitely masculine physique and personage,

Created tempted sparks on her magic stick,

She tried all juicily leering feminine trick,

But her desire-lorn curves in the air

Brought only pearly tears in those eyes fair,

Helplessly she came down,

and sat in front of him

with those rose-red lips pursed in a

heart-breaking frown,

Her nymphatic eyes were lost

in the handsome sculptural face,

On it there was not a single worldly trace,

Mesmerized!

She lost the sense of night's flight!

Next day!

The sun rose with full earthly delight,

Her eyes ogled at it terrified,

The hope to return to her realm died,

She'd broken the law of her place,

by not returning the same night

after that brief terrestrial, nocturnal brace,

The realization crashed at her

like a thunderbolt!

Her utmost sensuous bare shoulders

heaved under the tremors of this fault,

A heart-rending shriek escaped her throat,

And serenely flowing meditative phase

met this sinful, fullstopping dot,

His communion with the divinity broken,

and his aeonically closed eyes opened,

Even flora-fauna realized

something terrible had happened,

His fiercely burning eyes

stared at the petalous flower in sobs and sighs,

Her large flooded eyes pleaded for mercy,

But fire in his eyes was unforgivingly cursey,

His fabric of serenity was torn,

He thundered,

'Become an ugly bush of thorn!'

Mowed down by the spell of his cursing energy,

an ugly bush stood in place of those

beautiful limbs that kissed the air,

All shaken and ravaged he left the place,

A thorn branch, meanwhile, got entangled

in his loin cloth

as if for some meek, pleading brace.

He but scornfully jerked it apart,

and headed to some other place

for a new start,

Seasons then changed,

Spring's colorful patterns were rearranged;

Summer's warm kisses melted the snows;

Autumn's harvest fell to the air's chiding blows;

Winter's snowy blanket covered the peaks;

Rains lashed down in stormy freaks,

But this pleasant wavering of nature

couldn't shake the sage

from his meditative maze,

There faraway down the hills,

The accursed bush

shrouded in thorny haze,

struggled to sprout fruits and flowers,

How can something having a fairy core

remain thorny and ugly for too long?

Her beautiful soul entombed

in that thorny shrine prayed with penance,

Lo! A flower of her fruits sprout forth,

It was the day when the enlightened sage

arrived there from the north,

Contended with his cosmic realization

he came down the beautiful dale,

Passed as he that bush, his purified soul

sensed the shrub's throaty wail,

His feet disobeyed him and didn't move,

The flower fell at his feet,

in holy-most obeisance and greet,

He picked it up

and was lost in its beautiful smell,

What contradiction! Both exist together:

Flowery heaven and the thorny hell,

The latter due to his cursing condemnation,

The flower due to the beauty behind thorny bars,

Nasty worldly realization it was!

Hadn't he broken the beautifully set laws?

He bid penance at the altar for a long time,

His repenting self set around a reformative chime,

When his soul had'n salvaged of the sin,

Nobody could bet against her for a win.

There she blossomed out in front of him,

Beauty, charm and grace filled to the brim,

Her smile was forgetting and forgiving,

Inside the stony walls of his heart,

a new luminosity was now thriving,

And the elevated sage embraced her,

She who had'n separated from her loved ones

got the earthling she had fallen for,

Happiness, bliss and calm opened a new door

to the start of a new cycle of life, love and humanity.

All but the sage had'n extinguished by cataclysm,

The lone and forlorn survivor, he had'n tonking

at the doors of heaven with his questions,

Now they lived as a husband and wife,

New hopes, aspirations and offsprings

began to thrive!

Thus were sown the seeds of

another spell and cycle of life,

As their unchecked love in those

flowery vales left countless, exotic trails,

Gurgling brooks gave company

to her primordially sensuous laughter,

His instinct's procreating sprouts

mingled in the mirthful waters of her receptiveness.

The Parrot and the Old Sparrow

After a long, hard, heavy, wearisome journey

at sun down,

its will a bit cast down

and temper with a little frown,

The parrot with wings tired,

its beautiful colours all mired

in hard journey's perspiration

landed on a branch.

Winter was at its peak,

And anxious, drooping, panting was the beak,

With every minute saffron slanting rays

were melting into misty bays,

Cold was slowly creeping up

and its pinch was becoming bold

to take everything in its hold,

With sad eyes it ogled at the setting sun,

Too long and taxing had'n the run

and long forgotten was the flight's fun,

(Where was that fleeting, winged pun?)

With each mile the journey had become a drag

and vigour and energy that uplifted him with a brag

were now dumped in some pit,

Last ounce of strength was then hit,

But still he had far to go,

while his elevation became continuously low,

Before the eventuality did he bow

and anchored his feathery weight

upon a branch's restful bait,

'Merciless, frost-fanged will be the night,'

he thought to his misery's delight,

As the warmth vapoured off his body,

Shudder came over him with incremental ease,

Anxiously he ruffled his feathers

as if to loosen cold night's siege,

Where to spend the night

he thought from depression's highest heights,

Suddenness of sunset made him realize

the possible utility of the remaining time,

And he looked around like

the feeble truth emanating from a sad rhyme,

For miles long everything appeared

surrendered to the twilight's imminent pal,

And all wood appeared solid and creviceless;

without that niche which is a bird's hall,

Before his despair and agony touched another peak,
he heard a muffled, breaking-free, old, juvenile shriek,
An old sparrow,
its grayish patches long under time's harrow,
was seen bathing in a puddle,
Seeing him his senses went into a chilly huddle,
'Hey, such a cold night in waiting!
Take care it does not become death's baiting!
Fellow, you must take care
and must not extend your dare
to the extent of your doom!'
The sparrow squeaked and shrieked with zoom,
'My old coat has enough room
for the water to turn vapours
and shun and beat death's creepers!'

With his saggy, drenched feathering

the sparrow flew to him for a hearing,

And the visitor's problem was told,

Said the sparrow becoming gracious and bold,

'Dear, I have no family

and live in a banyan crevice,

Come with me, I'm at your service!'

It was a horribly chilly night,

No light for miles to sight,

Chilly rainstorm beat against the tree

to uproot the shackles and set it free,

But the tree was strong,

It withstood the deathly throng.

'I live here all alone,

Though reminiscences sometimes come to moan

over my beautiful, active past,

Darted when I fast

and voowed damsel sparrows with finesse,

Raised families as the cost for my instinct's ecstasies,

Then age caught with me,

Now eyes no longer see

the beauties of this world around,

but sense the death's bloodthirsty hound.

Still I live happily as the tail-end

of that great life lived,

Enjoyed I the choices that fate sieved,

Now, I have to pick up and play

among those things and chaff discarded

which remain unwanted above

as the fine particles trickle below,

Steadily this discarded heap grew

While I enjoyed the sieve's fine brew,

Now I roll like a kid in that rubble of the past

which was once waylaid by the youth's blast,

It now becomes the precious wealth

of my old age,

Shiny becomes the rage in this haze,

There are no takers for it now,

So I enjoy it all alone

without that competition's drone,

Happily I'm all alone with my age old,

And try even to become bold

against this winter's hold,

During youth I flew majestically high

To beat cold by my blood warmth,

But now wisdom swarmth,

And I still find ways

to brightly lit my days with these feeble rays,

In this cosy wood-hole of mine

Drunk I'm with my age's vintage wine,

I know that I may not go out of this hole

to ride softly on time's back at some dawn,

When mortality may pick up the pawn,

Leaving this old feathering engraved

in this very woody niche,

But that does not make me sick,

Because that sleep does not seem

different from the one that I now enjoy,

The pitcher of desire no longer exists,

Neither is it empty

so that I must have desires to have it full,

Nor it is full, so that I should browbeat

being afraid of losing it,

The sinews holding life to my body

have become impassive, senseless and bloodless,

They will not feel the pain of cleavage:

It will be just like an autumn leaf

being painlessly windblown into oblivion,

In this tepid existence of mine,

devoid of both heat and cold,

warmth and coolness prevail in some

pleasant, vague proportion,

Pleasure and pain seem to have lost their specificities:

Neither both exist, nor are they dead.

You are young and colourful!

How come you look so submissive and sad?

Have the conditions been so bad

to steal and rob all the real charm

and leave the colour on the feathers and soul

so dull and poor?'

The parrot spoke:

'Though I am young

but the spirit seems to have sung

the last song of life,

Too much has been the pain and strife,

My spirit seems to have run dry now,

Though the colour on my feathers holds somehow,

When just a hatching, father was gone,

Grew I hearing mother's moan,

The paternal sun thus never shone,

Still the biggest consolation was mother's

caressing, preening, feeding beak,

Ate I fruits at love's supreme-most peak,

As the sole nestling

I was fattened on her labours daylong,

And then went to sleep hearing her lullaby song,

Aha! Sweetest dreams came with a throng!

My whole existence was tethered

to that maternal pole,

The brightest, attractive-most star sole!

Under her great grooming,

colours on my feathering came bright,

Lavishly they flashed as I fluttered

them for my first flights,

Unbelievable was the pride and compassion

as her soaring soul's maternal shades

touched the brightest heights,

In her eyes I saw a new light,

How marvelous was that sight!

Alas her incorruptible love of yore

was arrowed by the fatality's shot,

Again cupid's arrow came hot,

I became a past with negligence and rot,

She was now in another spring of love,--

Incipient love for the future in her womb,

I thus became an orphan

even though my parents lived,

After many cries and

anguished aimless flights bereaved,

Life's burden with my soft feathers I heaved,

Young and beautiful, flew I with

time's oblivion and balm,

Intoxicating is such youth's charm.

Inevitably I fell in love,

Heartfully I cooed my beautiful lady,

Those love-lorn days when the heart

was ever ready to sing an ecstatic ditty,

Such a wealth was in my kitty,

So sweet, silent, mirthful, unencumbering

were those acceptances of nuptial responsibilities,

Those watchful, eager searches for niches

in trunks for our nest,

Tirelessly we wandered around for the best,

Guided by the love's brace

we found our place,

In some tiny hole

nothing else but we had all the role,

Our identities melted into each other,

How proud was I when I became father,

I'll not become like my parents, I thought,

I will not be ensnared like they were caught,

So I clung to my possessions with pride,

But the inevitability came with a chide,

In full bloom of youth and colours

all of my brood flew away,

My lady-bird came to be infatuated

under someone's cooing sway,

It was another fine day

when she bade adieu and flew away,

I embodied all forlornness,

All my loss was glaring in my face

monstrously unremedied,

I decided to leave that place,

And my sulking wings did brace

to take up the longest possible flight

from the place where such unfaithfulness abound,

So flew I as if pursued by

fearsome-most flying hound,

For many days I have been flying

with my soul aching and wings crying,

Why should we enter into something

and love somebody so completely,

if it is bound to go into gutters,

Isn't all such temporary dives

into life all banal?

Aren't we cogs in the hands of those

inevitable, unstoppable processes?'

The old sparrow, full of wisdom,

Undisputed king of his life's kingdom,

Spoke with the solace and simplification of age,

When youth's dilemmas no longer

haunt with their pinch and rage.

The sparrow said:

'It's just like a flower ruing

and weeping over other blooms,

because its beauty will not last forever

and will go to the glooms,

Dear, it's not we who are the ends,

Rather the beautiful phenomena like

love, marriage, procreation that decide the trends,

We are just the means to these

beautiful ends and destinations,

So, become a tool uncomplaining,

tilling earth without any expectations,

It is not that love exists

because we do love someone,

Love is the primordial sea without any

limits of space, time and individualities,

It is we who sweeten a few

moments of life with it,

till the chaotic, destructible existences get hit,

Do we procreate to cling to procreation life long?

No! We are made to procreate

to become unselfish means for the propagation,

for handing over the batons,

to perpetuate these beautiful phenomena of

love and relationships,

We do not leave behind an offspring,

but a possible instrument

which might come in handy for

the sustenance and survival of

those very precious moments

that got us the taste of love, happiness

and contentment at their best,

And if we recognize that

then our spirit gets a solacing rest,

If not,

then caught in the web of selfish net,

we acrimoniously bet

that I completely loved her

and became the cause of young lives,

It was I who caused that buzzing in those hives,

But such limitations would have been

meaningful had our survival unlimited,

or say our immortality was uninhibited,

But our journeys are to be ended,

So just cherish those moments that you tended,

If you cling to these phenomena

like they are your inheritance forever,

They become a drag around your neck,

making you a prisoner behind the bars,

which you create around yourself,

Liberate fella! Liberate yourself!

Become a journeyman who understands that

young flowers on a plant,

young soots on a twig

do not lessen themselves or the spring,

in not ruing over their wispy autumnal dismantling,

for they inculcate phenomena,

They help perpetuate nature

And they sustain the beautiful,

natural concepts of beauty and bloom,

They also served in a similar way,

made some new ray (though it is only light)

to decimate in some shadows, some gloom.'

The long fabric of the stormy night

was slowly lifted over their head,

Outside, stormy chilliness was fleeting

before a promising twilight,

Chances were there for a day bright,

Clouds parted from the face of the sky,
The parrot's spirits cut through the shadows
and soared high,
The old sparrow said:
'The day today is warm and sunny,
The dawn promises sweet honey,
Youngman, I'm in hurry to come out of my hole
and play my chirpy role
in the beautiful stage set around,
My soft soufflés and feeble light in my eyes
are enough even for the down-hilly afternoon,
You but go high,
because the forenoon is there for you,
with its multi-hue,
Go, so that you do not rue over

the day aimlessly lost,

Do justice to the old spirit of thy host,

Take some lesson from my soft feebleness

and the way I make a day out of my night.'

Thanking him the visitor flew away

into those swathes of promise,

where new life, new love, new relationships

held sway!

Platonic Love-making

These are the offsprings
of our platonic love-making,
I leave them in the
safe confines of your womb.
Nurture them!
Bear the pain of carrying
these restless, crying babies
inside your beautiful, safe self.
I am a weak father,
and you a strong mother,
You will need to
learn to be painless,
Because these burning babies of mine
are the angry fires
of their father's pyre.
The pyre in which the soft flesh of
the heart burns days in and days out.
You have been making love on the
hellish bed of my pyre
in which my living self burns forever.
In the fiery cradle
you have to hatch these cubs
of a father gone to ashes.

You have to blossom
living flowers amidst this
smouldering heap of
bones, flesh and my soul!

Torrents of Love

Your lip-kissed lies are

the diamonds of truth for me,

Forgive me my blindness;

Lost in your dream, reality I cannot see!

An old orchard!

Swathed in the peaceful shades

of meditative trance,

Wise old trees,

Ripe fruits hanging languidly,

Solitary footpath covered with

pale fallen leaves,

Moments mating with timelessness,

Then suddenly a gust of free breeze!

Pining storm!

Ruffled leaves!

Sighing branches!

And the fruits ripened from ancient times,

Fell under the spell of

those majestic shoves

unleashed by the free wind!

It was a cave!

Dark, dreary and cold!

And he was the yogi,

Immersed in an unending trance

impregnating silent, still moments.

Mossy, damp, dark!

Then a softly shining

raylet sneaked in!

Unleashed a storm of light!

It kissed the darkest,

inaccessible stony crevices,

Sucked out the lifeless

core of the dispirited self.

Those wispily pining lips exhaled

love, life and spirit!

It was pleasant riot!

An effusive mayhem!

An exhilarating melting!

An exciting massacre!

Of freedom over bondage!

Of light over dark!

Of............................

Summits stood proud,

Flaunting their rocky citadels,

'We are the unconquerable

Mountains,' they proclaimed,

A wild river came

with its riveting fury.

Its sharp, serpentine curves

let out throbbing, pulsating fury,

which cut through

the iron-hard rigidity.

Rocks gave in!

Summits after summits fell,

Their proud mass melting

in those sensuous swirls!

The river flew majestically

carrying boulders and sand

of those fallen soldiers who

challenged its majestic mirth.

Across the darkish cloud of my being,

You shine like a moon.

Milky......soft!

Beloved! You put this shining

signature on my being!

Wild river!
Feel the sand that you carry
in your majestic swirls!
That's me the proud mountain!
But that self was rocky and rigid,

Now I'm soft and cradled
in your gushing torrents!

****

Majestic river,

Now I feel like a

particle of sand

in the sensuous swathes

of your gushing waters!

In the pining silence of

frozen, dark hours,

a star spreads its mystic light

over a vacant heart.

Feminine raylets mate with

cold stones and impregnate

the boundless womb with

countless little stars.

The heart now becomes a galaxy,

It's self enlarged with a cosmic quotient

and profound peace spreads

across its bosom!

I am the moth

and I love my flame!

My fire!

But I feel the burning core of

the glow around which

I helplessly circle around!

I know that I cannot stop

the fire from burning,

So I throw myself in a fiery pit

to forget my dear flame's burning plight!

I throw myself in a bigger fire

so that I forget myself

and my flame's cries!

I feel the shapeless mass of your love,

It creeps like a venomous reptile

through the garden of my heart,

It furiously hisses,

returning my softest kisses,

I bear the toxic marks

left on my skin by your fangs.

Still I carry your poisonous bulk

in the soft cradle of my heart.

Why?

Because I have no choice to hate you,

I can just love you!

Love, I'd a cemented identity,

It was narrow, confined,

and constricted by the iron mask

put on my true face

by the society and circumstances.

The you walked in my life

with your pining majesty!

Your soft lips kissed the

the lifeless iron of my mask.

It melted in the softly smoldering

furnace of your pout!

The melting mask!

Its glowing fluid shining on my true face,

Beloved, you salvage my

real self from that imprisonment!

This real self may be good or bad

for the society,

For they judge by my identity old,

I but care not

because at least I see my true face!

There was an ice block,

As old as anyone can recall!

It had its frigid polar existence.

In the deep recesses of

its cold, snowy being,

endless nights pined,

Icy cage around its soul!

Then a warmth suddenly sneaked in!

Mossy rigidities melted under

the spell of those nimble cuts

and the stony ice melted,

Unleashing countless rivulets

gushing over his melting landscape.

The cage was broken,

The spirit merged in the

melodious embrace of

those royal-hued rays.

He lost his old self

to merge in a larger identity.

It was rebirth!

It was liberation!

The Stone and Dead Wood

Only a flower that has been allowed to blossom
knows the pleasures of caresses and kisses,
A stone but misses the breeze's deft touches,
Into its hardened pores no raylet reaches,
Only a beautifully blossomed bough
adorned with new shoots, saplings, leaves and flowers
dances to the air's singing tune,
A dry twig is all but immune to the storm's fury
and soft breeze's flirtatious games.
I too now become a stone,
Put me in desert's parched sand
and you will listen no moan,

Put me in the cosy confines of a luxurious room,

And you will hear no heart's boom,

Because all the juices vanished

during those nights of gloom.

A stone is a stone, is a stone, is a stone,

It has got its solid, concrete, lifeless status alone,

Inside it the light never shone

and its ironed particles clumped inseparably and forlorn.

Now, I too become a stone,

So let the storm blow,

It but cannot beat me further low,

Or let there be spring around,

Let the blossoms all panorama surround,

It but cannot change my face,

On my stony, statued lips no smile's trace,

A stone statue now I become,

Expressionless and eternally mum,

But the stone statue is not dead,

Even though no calamity's fear

roaming inside its ahead ,

and no pleasant expectation imprinted

anywhere in those cold stormy eyes,

But life somewhere deep down in its

solid chambers impassively sighs!

The Old Moon and the Imperiled Panorama

Pallid rays of this pale moon

had grown old so soon

during that half hour before the morning twilight,

It was a chilly, clear-skied, frosty, fogless January night,

The moon just a night away from fullness

had been exceptionally bright.

Nightlong, almost near the acme of its beauty

it had fulfilled its luminous duty,

Its milky beams had over-lighted

or overshadowed many a star,

It seemed eager to blot out

every stain and tainting tar,

Its beams falling like snows

upon sleeping horizon to the far,

The beautiful plains of this countryside

were lying in sleepy abundance

under the milky, chilly blanket with slumberous pride,

Everything was open to this celestial torch

with nothing to hide,

Cold-basking fields were huddled under their croppy sheets;

above was gloating the marvelous moon-shine,

Wheatlings stood bow-headed in reverence

with dewy crown fine,

Those marigold flowers were shining

unabashed under the milky showers,

The flowers happy about

losing their colors to the lover's

mysterious smiles and its powers,

White pea flowers boasted their augmented whiteness,

Aha, such dolefully beneficent had been the brightness,

Even trees didn't seem dark, indistinct specters

lurking shadowy over the horizon,

They appeared boats of foliage

floating in a misty sea,

In the background of such a brightly lit stage

even the sky seemed earth-lorn,

Through the milky transparency

its bluish-black veil lurked and through it

only the brightest stars smiled,

Scattered in the docile swathes of this

moon-baked countryside

villages seemed like mammoth ships silently

floating in the white wavy sea of light.

The moon was now well past its prime,

as if in shining too bright it had committed a crime,

Its setting quarter was in the north-west,

where the moony panorama had shone at its best,

And now it was moving towards rest,

Its strength and vigor had

dangerously plummeted down,

It now seemed ogling with a

meek, angry, anguished, helpless frown,

Its brightness was rapidly fading out

And its yellowish pale rays

appeared eager for a wailing shout,

Glumly it was fading over that sandy undulation

carrying fields, furrows, crops on its gently unfolding dome,

Shiny fruits born of sweat-laden efforts in its sandy loam,

Accusingly the moon threw pale, protesting

shadows in south-east,

where urbanism, consumption and crass commercialist

blatantly had its seat commanding, metropolitan, capitalist feast,

The area had been earmarked

for some merciless development project,

It now being defined by a tiny space

bound in a map issued under

the state government's gazette notification,

What a mischief by the developmental hand!

Ever eager to bulldoze over the nature

and turn it into uncomplaining, lifeless sand,

where lustrous stones will be built over the nature's burial,

Oofs! How heartless, wanton and depraved!

This pale, mournful moon

which was to set soon

into the misty gloom of twilight,

when a bright sun of consumerism and commerce

was ascending to its dawning height,

Those stalks of reeds

which sway in the cold breeze without greeds

seemed gently bidding the moon a good-bye,

Plummeted which further down

with a swollen face and a sigh,

Its pallid face grimacing with a painful nostalgia,

Its fading, setting rays tainted with deadly paleness;

Its oblong, teary face

now looked at this landscape,

Sleepy fields, warmthful wastes and fallow lands,

What mighty lessons have been taught here!

Aha! The farmer going to the fields with his gear,

Those long, painful, sometimes fruitless days

subsided when the sun's eager rays

looking at the sweat's trove

and the shirt's hoe,

Where the long painful dark nights

arrived like the deeds accomplished,

Where the failures galore

but the hard work never bored,

These failures defined success

as the losses stood just as a testimony to the profits,

Where hopes, aspirations and desires

varied with the changing hues of weather,

Farmer pawning everything

for the feathers in destiny's crown,

Gold forms immaterially—

or minimally at the rate of a dust speck for a gram—

in the toiled soil brown,

All will be gone,

The moon was also dying with a moan,

This beautiful charming mystery of the landscape—

why hardest labour fetches minimal returns;

and why a bit less harder toil results in

a soul-satisfying speckful of return that seems wealthiest—

All this beautiful, aesthetic, curvy, circuiting strings;

Mysteries of landscape, of destiny,

of the see-saw battle between pleasure and pain,

between penury and sustainable as well as gluttonous gain,

between life and death:

All this will be lost for a direct, straight,

materially penetrating needle of surety,--

The commercial, unflinching and fixed

use of the landscape

in the form of concrete approach

where profits will boomerang

in proportion to the short-cuts;

Where compromised morality, ideology and conscience

will not face any ifs and buts;

Where there will not be any sweet scent

of labour that will be replaced by

the mechanical, greasy, muddy panting

of merciless competition and grab;

Where concrete blocks, flats will replace

these wonderous solitudes basking in and around;

Where sheaves, stalks, straw and reeds

will not sway to the breeze,

but blank, rigid, ironed tower

will stand mutely, inflexibly to the nature's cooing calls.

Now the sorrowfully yellowing

death rattle of the setting time

was arriving with a chime.

There on the opposite horizon the day opened a window

to sneak a peek at the imperiled room of the night,

Wispily, there was the twilight

with its mixed day-night delight,

In its mysterious lap,

the old moon met a slightly premature death,

Slumped as it feebly, freely

into the silvery sea of mist

standing still over the treeline.

Into this sea of death, the moon plunged,

And the twilight mischievously winked

with it unfaithful, teasing look asking favours

both from the night and the day,

The old moon was gone with its last ray,

And soon-to-be-doomed panorama,

unmindful of the fatality waiting,

came out of its dewy slumber,

A crane's clarion call

cree....ked over its yawning breast,

The sun prepared to cast its first ray

and the fields got up for another hard farming day.

PS—Time of the poem: Half hour before the morning twilight of January 13, 2006 (Lohri); a day before the full moon day (Makar Sakranti, January 14).

Conversation with a Stranger

One day he asked someone hiding inside

the bodily façade like a fugitive,

'Who are thou?

And why despite all the architectural negativities

people define thou positively?'

From its unreachable deep cellar

that someone raised its germ-free, disinfected voice,

'I am the exiled one without choice,

While the bones and the flesh around me

in worldly spotlight rejoice,

I just take the ordained backseat

and watch the game of

birth, survival, struggle and death

played inside the castle on the shaking stage.'

'Don't you feel perplexed by the passing days?'

Again the query was voiced,

'Don't you feel bad or ever you rejoiced?'

It answered in a heavy, impassive tone,

'Thy gimmick cannot shake my throne,

In the timeless shades I spend my time here

and when the castle will be broken

the death squad will find the door open,

Away I'll fly with the figures of

deeds and misdeeds to the final court,

and if it is found short,

again I'll be exiled.

It has been like this for thousands of years,

but I never rejoice at new birth

nor weep at death and shed tears,

My book lies in mighty primordial hands

and the player to settle scores

changes with worldly trends,

I am the same forlorn, exiled child

of the majestic, mighty father,

It's a never-ending game perhaps,

A tiny cog on the chessboard of creation,

Let's see how high and mighty you make the castle,

Void will then gobble the tone and stars!'

9 798887 041421

Printed by Libri Plureos GmbH in Hamburg,
Germany